SHREWD MARKETING
Marketing Artifices of the 21st Century

SHREWD MARKETING

Marketing Artifices of the 21st Century

Pranav Kumar

ANMOL PUBLICATIONS PVT. LTD.
NEW DELHI - 110 002 (INDIA)

ANMOL PUBLICATIONS PVT. LTD.
4374/4B, Ansari Road, Daryaganj
New Delhi - 110 002
Ph.: 23261597, 23278000
Visit us at: www.anmolpublications.com

Shrewd Marketing: Marketing Artifices of the 21st Century

First Published, 2006

ISBN 81-261-2580-2

PRINTED IN INDIA

Published by J.L. Kumar for Anmol Publications Pvt. Ltd., New Delhi - 110 002 and Printed at Mehra Offset Press, Delhi.

A

Tribute to

Mom and Dad

Preface

Shrewd marketing enables you to learn the most practical implications of marketing theories and principles. This is pragmatic. For example, there are many large consultancy firms who fetch benefits to organizations through a clever and wise financial planning, by letting them know as to how to take advantage of accounting and taxation related aspects. Similarly, in business, the big firms follow shrewd marketing practices which is suggested by the same so called top consultants, which can be experienced anytime by the marketers operating in upcountry markets. Killing your competitors silently, marketing people's selling tricks during closings or during bad performances (by motivating the electrical engineer for making rapid fluctuations in the voltage so as to result in damage of many lamps/bulbs in the region ,that ultimately influences the demand of the lamps and the already prepared marketer fulfills this demand and gets his sales figure achieved) etc. are some of the examples of Shrewd Marketing. Shrewd marketing is practised secretly and it can not be understood easily by everyone unless it is learnt properly.

Traditional marketing has become out dated, accepts even Philip Kotler.The success of any organization depends upon its adroitness at Shrewd Marketing.

The book explains the concept of Shrewd marketing through many SM (Shrewd marketing) strategies elaborated in a lucid manner. You can now understand how companies are successful in different industries by exploiting SM strategies in a hyper-competition era. The names of the companies have not been mentioned on their request, as they want to continue practicing it silently.

Shrewd Marketing strategies make you aware of the different market influencing forces; you are suggested not to go for any wrong, objectionable or unethical step; instead it is aimed at making you careful so that no one can throw you out of the business. Shrewd Marketing guides you in understanding all the pleasant and unpleasant marketing activities being practised in recent times by the leading organizations globally for assured success.

Pranav Kumar,
Faculty, Marketing

Contents

Shrewd Marketing Foundation

The basics of Shrewd marketing lie in the fact that how successful organizations conduct their marketing activities and how they simultaneously ascertain that competitor's marketing activities fail. And this ascertainment of the failure of competitor's moves is nothing but Shrewd Marketing.

Traditional marketing strategies guide you to play dead moves; shrewd marketing teaches you to play deadly moves. It is a marketing practice adopted by the leaders to beat their competitors through proper study, action and control over different levers of markets in a totally shrewd manner. They induce the customers into buying their products cleverly; they make channel partners work like anything by properly understanding and cleverly satisfying their genuine and non-genuine needs. The firms using SM strategies hire with respect the best marketing people who are in form at present and fire without mercy who have been unable to perform recently.

A successful firm always plays dangerous moves so as to destroy the marketing intentions of the followers even before it is implemented, or when it is being implemented or after it is implemented.e.g. in confectionaries industry, a small firm spends a good sum on advertisement to get some more business in a season. But after they have advertised heavily according to their permissible budget, a big firm deliberately causes some adulteration in the product of this small firm through some of its loyal and good retailers. Now when the customer buys it, the adulteration is caught and it spoils the whole advertisement results that were expected to be derived because the big firm publicizes it properly through either by coming in the limelight or without letting its name come into the picture.

Now if you are from a big firm You have to play these kind of deadly moves and if you are a small or newer firm, you have to learn these moves to protect yourself. Thus you have to learn it anyway, does not matter you are big or small.

A firm has to continuously evolve the techniques to ruin its competitor's marketing moves if it is to increase its market share. The marketing results of other firms can be worsened and that of yours can be ameliorated through different SM (Shrewd Marketing) Strategies explained throughout the book which is divided into five Shrewd Marketing levels depending upon the complexities involved and; adroitness required for the proper understanding of its applicability, suitability and credibility for an organization. It is recommended to create a safety network for you in the industry by understanding it properly. If you do so, no one would be able to pose a threat to your business; it is never suggested to go for any unethical business practice.

Shrewd Marketing Level I

1. THE CUSTOMER IS PROSTITUTE

One can not have the best possible impact of one's marketing strategies unless the behavior of the customer is supposed to be similar to that of a prostitute. There was a time when marketers used to call customers god, king, dictator and what have you of this. It was the customer who decided the fate of the product through its different behavioral patterns. Excellent features and good quality ensured the sustainability of a product if other marketing factors were controlled wisely. Now the time has totally changed and customers have many options in a perfectly competitive market whose basic features are presence of many sellers and buyers, products having similar attributes, price uniformity etc. Setting customer oriented strategies is really a herculean task at a time when leaders are facing competition from the big as well from the small firms at global, regional or local level and when the followers are finding it difficult to survive with the universal objective of profit making (although they may have to go with certain social obligations as well, if they really want to succeed in their primary motive of more profits; the more profit you want to make, the more affectation you will have to have of being socially responsible —this is what successful companies do, but tactfully).

Today's customer is completely behaving like a prostitute. The customers off late quickly go for a brand that gives them more benefits. Even for a marginal betterment, they do not hesitate in switching to other brands; moreover they are constantly more and more demanding. In case you are able to satisfy them, they will buy your product; the day someone else comes up with a changed outlook or offers products with simple additional benefits, they will go for this new product. The expectations of the customers are touching sky these days. Fashion, preferences etc. are taking no time in getting totally changed. That is why the customers now, without any exception, always want the products with latest and trendy features. Every industry is being guided by this rule of business.

Therefore, in order to understand & satisfy a customer you will have to think literally that how to satisfy a prostitute, who's demands are ever rising. One has to successfully try to make some value addition in one's product for every next time a customer comes to buy one's product. The basic idea is—to cater today's customers properly, like your strong rivals, you will have to meet continuously changing customer's demands based on latest trends; sometimes you may have to go ahead of the time in terms of innovativeness & continuous product development; you need to go for accelerated marketing activities every now and then and it should be tried to have a sharp look over competitor's moves so as to develop attacking strategies through Shrewd marketing.

2. ONE'S ADVERTISEMENT, OTHER'S BENEFITS

(How to use other's advertisement in your favour)

These days companies are spending a huge sum on the advertisements. But many share the actual advantage of the advertisement made by a particular organization. Suppose in the field of education, there is a coaching institute preparing students for different competitive examinations. This institute is having its branches and franchisees in different cities of a country. Now this institute is trying to increase the market share. For this purpose it decides to go for heavy advertisement as per the permissible budget. Now that advertisements are done, the target customers start feeling the need and those who were already feeling the need start searching for the brands that can deliver them best. Although advertisement was made by the firm in discussion, but the target customers start looking at all the options available in the accessible market. During this process, a shrewd firm (which has actually not given this advertisement) improves its quality and features in its offerings. And the moment a customer comes, he is offered prompt and comparatively better designed solutions, as a result he finds the shrewd firm's product behooving and ultimately goes for it. That is how you can use other's advertisements in your favour. Just take care of the nature of products you are dealing in and whenever some advertisement appears by your rivals, get your seat belts tightened and respond with alacrity by quickly making some cost effective and feasible improvements / modifications in your products.

3. UTILISING THE BEAUTY FACTOR IN BUSINESS

There are many industries like automobile, show business etc. where the beauty factor is utilized to a great extent in promotions. In auto advertisements, it is very easy to find women wearing attractive clothes, they start dancing with style when a visitor comes to the car being promoted. Just the money is paid and a dramatic effect is obtained that adds immense value to the existing marketing efforts being undertaken. They can welcome your guests with purchased smile at hotels, at airports, in offices, board rooms etc. In sales, women have been performing reasonably well off late because they have the ability to convince & to appeal vehemently the professionals, the governments and the masses. Try to find out the applicability and suitability of such hidden strengths in your business. These days, it is very common to find out the companies exploiting this factor properly for having more business coming up by flexibly adhering to the principle of business ethics.

4. CDS (COMPETITION DEMOTIVATORS) STRATEGY

(Deciding the marketing blend—a step forward from Marketing Mix)

McCarthy's four Ps—product, price, place and promotion convey the exact idea about different marketing aspects in an ideal situation. Today the marketplace has turned into a Chessboard where everyone is playing well thought shrewd moves. You can easily find out products around you that are not doing well although they have fine quality, they are competitively priced and they are promoted and distributed properly on regular basis. Earlier these steps were good enough for a product to succeed. Now these four factors have gotten an equally dominating colleague, which is known as "Competition Demotivator". Every successful organization is essentially guided by this and one has to keep on developing various Competition Demotivators time to time in order to suppress rival's marketing efforts. e.g. In packed drinking water industry, a company can claim that a particular rival company is filling the ordinary tap water in bottles. This will disturb the product stability, the market position and market share of that company for the time being and thus you get an opportunity to speed up your marketing activities to enhance your market share. This is a continuous exercise, so you have to continuously keep on devising the Competition Demotivators(CDs) applicable to your industry which is ultimately aimed at your competitors. These CDs may vary from industry to industry, company to company and they need to be updated on a regular basis to maintain the leadership status or to attain the leadership status, and most importantly to break the winning game of the existing leaders of the industry.

5. QUALITY COMPROMISE WITHOUT LETTING THE CUSTOMERS KNOW ABOUT IT (SOMETIMES IT IS DELIBERATELY MADE KNOWN)

You have to continuously update the features of your product. If you can not improve the quality, then change the packaging. Remember a simple girl when dressed well attracts many. Similarly even if the product is simple, present it in excellent manner. Leaders in this context adopt a unique SM strategy time to time by degrading the quality. Sometimes a little bit compromise / degradation in quality enables a marketer in initiating the price war. Customers would not understand initially that you have lowered the quality of the product; instead they will simply be amazed at your price reduction moves and would accept your product gladly. Your rivals will desperately follow your moves otherwise they will lose the market share. Today customer is more demanding. It seeks best quality at best price. Obviously the quality can not be afforded to be inferior, but a slight deviation from the fine quality reduces the cost of production and this move can not be easily understood by the customer. The customer will not understand it for the meanwhile in the industry like fast moving consumer goods, durables etc. While sometimes quality is degraded by letting the customers know about it, like in aviation industry, prices are sometimes decreased by admitting it very clearly that the particular services will not be provided. This can be seen quite often in the case of low cost airlines.

6. ATTRACTING RIVAL'S CHANNEL PARTNERS CLEVERLY AND MAKING THEM WORK FOR YOU (BY SHOWING EXAGGERATED RESPECT)

Channel partners play a significant role in the growth of an organization. They are highly influenced by the margins, commissions, schemes etc. being offered by the companies. Select the best Channel partner of your competitor, try to break his association from your rival and make him work for you ultimately. Remember, the channel partners are also entrepreneurs so they need profit as well as respect. Obviously every company will fetch them profits, you try to convince them in terms of respect. Tell the channel partners that they will be given certifications like respected business partner or primary / priority channel partner etc. signed by the Marketing Head. Give them the certificates and see how happy they are and see how happily they display the certificates at their respective premises. This is how top firms are dealing with their channel partners. Moreover, call them in meetings commend them for their performance and give them an opportunity to sit among top-notch professionals with whom they would not have been able to even talk otherwise. It motivates the intermediaries to a great extent.

7. DEMOTIVATING RIVAL'S WORKERS

These days it is very common to give interview offers to the competitor's employees for jobs having more salary and better perks and finally not selecting them. This is great enough to demotivate them. They start looking for other options immediately after this. The firm practicing it gets its purpose quickly solved as it badly affects the current performance of these employees due to lack of attention and due to lack of affinity with the current job. These employees start focusing more on job search than on the current job.

8. CHANNEL PARTNER'S SHREWD MANAGEMENT

Find out thoroughly the negative points of your competitors towards their channel partners like—delay in clearing different types of claims, inability to cater as per the schemes on time, failure in keeping the sales force happy, supply of more products to the distributors than actually demanded, delivery of non required products by the leading companies to the channel partners for selling compulsorily. E.g. when a top company in the fmcg industry introduces a new soap, it supplies this soap to all the channel partners, even though they are not willing to take it initially because their money may be jammed for the time being as it may not get the desired demand in the beginning. So, the shrewdness is to supply in this manner if you are a leader and; in case you are not a leader then train your sales people in a way that they keep on saying in the market that your organization does not exert unnecessary pressure on the intermediaries in this particular way, which means that you supply only those goods which have really been ordered by the channel partners. Meanwhile in both the cases your sales force will have to actually keep on exerting pressure for taking more and more orders for billings.

It has been observed that the leading companies make delays in settling the claims of their channel partners till a reasonable time; they keep on coming up with new schemes continuously and then they clear the earlier claims and leave pending the last one. This late settlement of the last claim and eagerness to listen about the next scheme play very important role in making the channel partners work for you like anything. This practice is a very commonly used exercise these days by the leading companies. In fast moving consumer goods industry it is very common to find it being practiced.

9. HIRING THE TOP PERFORMERS FROM YOUR RIVAL'S PLACE

Always hire the top performing employees from your rival's camp; make them work for you at any cost. The best strategic time to take them is when your rival company is going to speed up its marketing activities or going for new promotional measures in festive seasons etc. In this manner your two intentions get fulfilled—firstly, the top performers of the industry come to work for you; and secondly, your rival is disturbed at time when it was to take steps in new marketing dimensions. It is suggested to take the people from your competitors when they are trying for and going to deliver their best at your rival's place. The need is to identify the right timings for taking them at yours.

10. SENDING SMIC (SHREWD MARKETING INFORMATION COLLECTORS) TO THE COMPETITOR'S ORGANIZATION

When you have a doubt of new planning being done by your competitor in terms of product development, technology upgradation, formulation of new marketing strategies etc., you should send some of your marketing people to join your competitor at various levels. Let these SMICs (Shrewd Marketing Information Collectors) stay there till you know every ins and outs about the competitor's moves and then let them come to you one by one with the passage of time without coming in the knowledge of your competitor. You must have heard of many professionals coming back to their earlier organizations – is an example of SMICs. But at the same time beware of the SMICs sent by your competitors also to your organization by proper verification of every small to big detail about the new appointees in terms of experience and past record.

11. MOTIVATING THE COMPETITORS IN ATTACKING YOU IN WRONG AND USELESS DIRECTIONS

(Confusing the competitors through manipulated market research reports)

Today there are market research firms who keep on conducting surveys like – how many times women / men want to have sex in a week; who is concerned more for the children—father or mother; etc. These market research firms always / many times give you the results as you want. Now you develop your market information system in a way that you are always updated about the latest trends, behaviors and forecastings. And then learn to play the game with competitors. Suppose you have a report through a properly conducted market research that demand of a particular product is going to wane in the months to come. You act with shrewdness in the market by spreading the information that the demand is going to increase for that particular product rather than revealing the fact that the demand will actually decrease. The market research firm will make this report for money; that is not a problem these days. Second information you are spreading is that you are to expand your production limits so as to meet the increased demand; while actually you are not going to do it. This will ignite your competitors in understanding the matter definitely in an unclear way and they may decide to invest (actually misinvest); or they might stay confused because these reports would not match with the reports prepared by their own marketing intelligence system; ultimately they would land up with the problem of either overproduction or they may go for some improper marketing steps that may have umpteen ramifications. Similarly always keep on misinforming your rivals about the trends, about your strategies etc. It will always motivate them in attacking you in wrong and useless directions.

12. APPLYING INNOVATIVENESS AND CREATIVITY IN AN ENTIRELY DIFFERENT MANNER— CONTINUOUS MARKET PREDICTION STRATEGY

Always keep on predicting the markets for keeping you ahead of your competitors. Develop your plans as per the prediction, which would enable you in winning over the situation all the time. Moreover in the due course it will give you an expertise that even if market does not move according to your prediction, you would give direction to the market in terms of improved fashion, better products, product varieties etc. If these changes were to come according to your prediction, and you are ready to deliver the new demand, you emerge successful. But if market did not move as per the prediction then also you made available these new things in the market; that again attracts the customer and you are considered to be proactive and the whole market is bound to deliver on the same pattern initiated by you. This is how you attain the leadership position in any situation by applying your innovativeness and creativity through continuous market prediction strategy.

13. ALWAYS THINK BIG AND ALSO MAKE YOUR PEOPLE THINK BIG FOR A LARGER MARKET SHARE

When an ordinary company plans to enter into a new market, it studies the whole market potential properly. Then it comes to a conclusion that it can tap a low market share, suppose 10 to 12%. And it acts according to this target and tries to achieve this through combined efforts of every member of the organization. But when a smart company plans to enter a new market, it visualizes that it can capture a large market share that can vary from industry to industry. Suppose here it thinks of capturing 30% or 40% or 50% market share. It starts acting according to this target and every member of the organization is directed to achieve this target and they achieve it also if the plans work out well. But they could achieve it only because they thought big. You must have a wide vision and at the same time your employees should also be convinced/motivated enough so that there is a match between the organizational goal and the employee's goal. This will bring extraordinary results to your marketing efforts you plan to undertake, does not matter how difficult it is.

14. OFFERING PRODUCTS /SERVICES TO THE CHANNEL PARTNERS AT LESSER PRICES IN A SHREWD MANNER

Successful firms always keep on offering goods at manipulated prices (different prices for different intermediaries) to its channel partners through different techniques (although they don't disclose this trick as they always have some common and same price list and/or catalogue for showing it to the channel members). Those who give good sales are cleverly offered lesser prices. Distributors are always asked to order and take more goods for getting additional benefits. This additional benefit is an artifice extensively used by the marketers to enable the intermediaries in offering the product at lesser prices (than the price recommended by the sales people) to the retailers. This is happening in industries like fast moving consumer goods, durables etc. Even in financial product's sector the middlemen are given commissions / brokerages and what have you of this. These commissions are normally based on different slabs. Suppose a direct marketing associate bringing business to a housing finance company gets 0.25% commission on total business brought by him. In case he brings more business than a particular limit, he is entitled for a commission of 0.5%

up to another certain limit, beyond which he is entitled for a commission of 0.75%. These figures naturally vary from industry to industry. The point to be noted here is that this varying commission encourages the direct marketing associates in offering the product at manipulated prices. He manages to sell the products/services at lesser prices than that of the competitors because he is lessening the price by sacrificing some income that he would derive at the maximum slab. He works aggressively so as to reach to the highest slab as he gets maximum commission there; you always have an advantage because he remains motivated and works very hard this way, which he would not have done otherwise.

15. PRESSURISING CHANNEL PARTNERS AND SALES FORCE

It has been observed practically by the leading organizations that the intermediaries and sales force work well under pressure. Normally channel partners and sales force get commissions/margins and salary & performance based incentives respectively. If your sales staff keeps on pressuring the distributors and dealers to take and sell more and more, it brings different feelings in the minds of your channel partners. They normally think that this company is exerting excessive pressure; nevertheless they try to get more sales so as to earn more, because in business everybody wants to make maximum profits with sustainable growth. This temptation of making more money forces them to accept your pressure. Secondly, these intermediaries sell through the sales force of your organization, although they may or may not use their own sales men in many cases. So the basic idea is, the pressure of sales you exert on your intermediary is generally passed on to your sales people for the execution. Therefore you have to simultaneously put pressure on your sales force also for liquidating the goods of your channel partners in his territory. He will definitely accept the pressure, better say he has to accept it if he wants to stay. Always remember that sales and marketing people are the best paid professionals, but only if they achieve the targets. If they don't achieve the targets you will always get a better professional. Throw the non-performers and take new ones and carry them till they keep on tolerating pressure without losing performance. This is how leading firms are dealing with their sales and marketing professionals at every level—from sales Executive to Vice President. One should never compromise on these matters. There is no applicability of Japanese management principle of lifetime employment for the non-performers in the current scenario.

16. TO ADVERTISE A LIQUOR BRAND, ADVERTISE SOME OTHER PRODUCT OF THE SAME BRAND (CUSTOMER CLEARLY GET YOUR MESSAGE; YOU JUST UNDERSTAND THE CONCEPT)

There can be different types of legal restrictions for advertising alcoholic drinks or harmful products. In that case, develop a supplementary product with the same brand and advertise it that does not come under purview of legal restrictions. Your target customers will directly get the message and will catch the intention behind it. For example a liquor brand is advertised by advertising soda or packed drinking water with the same name. Other public relations exercise by these brands may include wishing the nations during festive seasons with the same name again. The customers get well communicated.

17. KEEP ON SEARCHING FOR CHEAPEST RESOURCES GLOBALLY

Today most of the quality brain is entering into the field of Information technology. See the top IT companies have heavily resorted to Business Process Outsourcing from the developing or underdeveloped nations in order to take advantage of the cheaper labor. There are countries where employees are required to work in the night shifts for these BPO firms that make them suffer from many insomniac and other diseases. The Shrewd Marketing suggests you to get your work done from anywhere, by remunerating the employees properly. Go on exploiting this strategy; see around you and you will find that every top company is doing this; at the same time SM suggests you to always keep on claiming that your human resource management is of world class. For example here, you should provide Gymnasium to these night awakening fellows, you provide them best food from the best hotels and see how happy they are. This is the tendency of a particular class of the people to get exploited in anyway for some money. You should always take the advantage of this. Similarly keep on looking for the cheaper sources of other resources also.

18. NEVER BE EMOTIONAL IN TAKING STERN DECISIONS

Successful organizations are never governed by emotions while taking stern decisions like sacking an employee, changing or modifying technology, shutting down of loss making units, shifting the manufacturing units from one place to another etc. Even public sector units also now do not like emotions and similar psychological aspects in business matters. For example whenever a company has to reduce the size of its workforce, it resorts to a very well accepted and well practiced shrewd strategy these days. A press release is given that this company is going to downsize its workforce and there are plans to remove say one thousand employees by next year. This kind of announcements you will find almost everyday in leading dailies by some or other companies. The intention behind this is to give the indication to the employees that they should start looking for other options. Enough care has to be taken while using this strategy because it sends a message to the employees that the condition of the company is not good or the company is unable to grow etc. So the current employees start concentrating more on job search than concentrating on their current job. Although it is normally aimed at removing the employees with lesser productivities, but sometimes even star performers also start looking for other options after these kind of decisions by the top authorities which ultimately fetches unwanted losses to the organization. So it is suggested to practice this kind of strategy in a very delicate manner having a sophisticated style of communication.

19. PROFESSIONALS—BRAND YOURSELF

It is a global phenomenon today. You as professionals have to go for self promotion time to time so as to position yourself as a strong entity in the industry. Gone are the days when only politicians, pop stars, Football players etc. used to brand themselves. Now if you promote yourself as a strong brand in the corporate sector, it helps your organization achieve an edge over competitors on many fronts. Remember there are people in the industry who have positioned themselves in a way that their being with an organization is a matter of prestige and privilege for the organization itself. When you are having a good brand image and many people know your name in the industry, your many tasks will get executed very easily at different occasions. This is the psychology of the people that they do the work fast and quickly for the famous people.

20. PREPARING THE CUSTOMERS IN ADVANCE FOR A PRICE HIKE

Whenever an industry is feeling the pressure of probable increases in the raw material costs, it becomes evident that the production costs are bound to increase. When the production cost rises, the price of the commodity will rise. This situation is quite common in almost every industry. The leading firms react to this situation in a very tricky manner. They start giving press releases (which actually intend to keep the customers ready for the price rise well in advance) to inform the public that there have been several rises in the raw material costs for quite some time; companies have been suffering so far; but if the situation continues, the price of the final product may be increased. Secondly, to collect some more sympathy of the customers it is also mentioned in the press release that the small firms in business will have to suffer severely on account of the rising raw material costs. This exercise is being repeated for some time and thus psychology of the customers does not remain with any choice than to accept the fact that the prices are going to be increased due to genuine reasons. And when the price of the product actually increases, customers accept it without much resistance. In some cases this strategy is used so adroitly that customers are found be even discussing about the probable price rises in future about a particular product /service. This strategy can be seen being used by maximum number of leading firms in different industries, more commonly in manufacturing industries. It is preparing your customer in advance to be amicably ready for a price hike.

Shrewd Marketing Level II

21. LOW PROFILE ENTRY STRATEGY

Low profile entry strategy is being used by the new firms or by the big organizations that enter into a market and want to operate without much hype and hoopla and by making proper and sustainable efforts. It has been seen being practiced significantly by the companies who have created a niche for themselves in spite of the presence of extremely strong players in the market. It so happens that the leaders have their own rules and they control their channel partners in their own style. You will not find every channel members happy in the market. They have their own grievances for the companies they are dealing with. If at this point of time a new player comes offering products with attractive benefits for the intermediaries, like comparatively better margins/commissions, good schemes which have full scope to be concealed from further passing on, strong back end, regular visits of the efficient sales people and timely settlement of claims etc., is warmly welcomed and gets a success which is unprecedented.

Remember, big firms can not practically keep their all channel partners happy, and small firms do not have resources to keep them totally happy, therefore there is always a room for the new players in the market who have an opportunity to cater these channel partners satisfactorily. To exploit this scope without much opposes from the leaders and competitors, low profile strategy is being used by various companies worldwide. The beauty of this marketing strategy is that by the time your competitors come to know about you as a threat, you have established yourself. And now the competitors will start thinking of attacking strategies, which is if implemented, will give you more publicity and that also at their cost. You just have to maintain the product's quality, an effective supply chain supported with a competitive price and the best schemes.

22. MARKETER'S SELLING TRICK DURING CLOSINGS OR DURING THE PERIODS OF BAD PERFORMANCES

The companies, which are working aggressively in the markets for having a lion's share, practice it very cleverly through several artifices. Most of the so called big intermediaries who give more business to a company, who have the capacity to take up more goods from the company during sluggish periods, who have the courage to share the burden of the salespeople during weekly,monthly,half-yearly and yearly closings, are given special type of incentives by the marketing people differently at different levels. For example lets talk of a lighting company operating in a country having divided its market in four regions—North, South, East and West. Now suppose the RSM (Regional sales manager), North wants the main distributors of his region which has four states each being led by respective AMs (Area Managers), to take the goods 20 % more in quantity this month. It is assumed that this excess stock will be proportionately transferred to the small dealers and retailers in that particular month by these distributors in their respective area of operations. Now the question is that why these distributors will take 20 % more in quantity when they will find good amount of difficulty in transferring the products in more than required quantity to the smaller intermediaries. The RSM of this Lighting company then asks the AM to give these distributors on account of damage and breakage a 1. 5% lump sum claim on the total billing of this month, which is 0. 5% more than the earlier 1% and that also was being given on actual verification of the damaged lamps. The damage report is prepared in the cabin of the distributor without going for the earlier method of verifying, counting and breaking the lamps. But in case the damage claims are made in advance and later on they come to know that there has been some actual damages also; that is also adjusted by the marketing people either in the same month or in the next month. The only important thing here is that the sales people have to keep in their mind that this special incentive should not allowed to be demanded by these intermediaries themselves in future. This is marketer's tool and not the distributor's rights. They can be lied that this has been permitted by the National Sales Manager himself so as to face the competitor's challenge this month or say this time it is the question of our boss's prestige so you have to take it; or say next month distributors performance appraisal is to go to the corporate office so you just need it for your recognition as a renowned business partner of the company; or say there is an indication that price can increase next month so it is the time to take more material and sell it at increased price; etc.

23. LEARN ENCASHING THE SCHEMES FOR INTERMEDIARIES BEFORE IT IS ACTUALLY INTRODUCED

The marketing people always have the idea about the promotional schemes that are going to be introduced in near future. These professionals should learn the ways to start manipulating the intermediaries about these schemes. The scheme will fetch more benefit to those who have performed well recently and who have the capacity to facilitate the growth of the company etc. — matters like these should be communicated to the intermediaries and they should be asked to enhance the sales, to speed up the selling activities and to intensify the penetration during this period. Intermediaries have a tendency to work harder for the availing of current as well as future schemes. Although the magnitude of their effort depend upon the ability of the sales people operating in the upcountry markets and the pressure techniques used by the bosses sitting at branch offices. Every big company starts encashing the schemes before it is actually launched through its marketing personnel.

24. FACILITATING INFILTRATION AT TIMES

This is a very important marketing tool for a company in a well controlled market. Every successful organization maintains its markets divided in different territories and regions, free from infiltration. It is so tried that the products of one territory does not enter into other territories. A dealer in a territory has to sell at a price decided by the company to its retailers and other intermediaries. Now if this dealer goes for rate cutting and starts selling at this price in his own territory then he will be caught by the sales people, so he enters into other territories through his known persons or relatives in that area or through developing direct contacts in unknown territories. This is how infiltration takes place mainly due to the fact that it is very easy to sell at a price which is lesser than the price offered by the local dealer. And it is the main motive considered to be behind the intermediaries going for infiltration. It is mainly the job of the sales people to check the materials going from one territory to another by regular market visits and by keeping regular track of stock of the dealers. But practically speaking, in recent times infiltration has emerged as a life saving tool for the sales personnel at lower, middle and at higher levels. Normally higher management does not permit this directly; they simply say the middle level to give a bigger sales volume anyhow. Sales is totally controlled by this term 'anyhow'. You have to sell anyhow—this is how you are instructed. So, normally lower level sales people force intermediaries to infiltrate in adjoining territories; while middle level sales personnel allow them to infiltrate into larger territories time to time as their targets are higher than that of lower level. But the middle level infiltration strategy is not allowed to be known to the lower level sales people and also not to the dealers to whom it was not allowed. You have to be ready to defend the infiltrating intermediaries cleverly in case the accusation comes which is bound to come. This infiltration strategy should not be used regularly like every month. Hiccup is required between two uses. This is an excessively and extensively used strategy by the top companies in any industry. Remember, if you go for this strategy carelessly and without studying the ways to control the ramifications, it can be disastrous. This marketing activity requires extremely sophisticated control measures.

25. TRYST BUILDING PUBLIC RELATIONS EXERCISE

When the multinational corporations start businesses in new markets in different countries, they adopt a common strategy. Each country is visited by the top executives and a press conference is arranged to communicate that this particular MNC is going to start operations in that country. Every good aspect of the country is praised and the customers of that country are well commended. Normally you will find every top executive saying almost same thing in these kind of visits, like—the people and the country have very high level of ethical values; it has vast market potential; the customers of this country are willing to pay for the quality products. etc. It is also heard to be saying that customer is king. Although the customers now know that at times they are offered objectionable carbonated drinks, objectionable potato fries & burgers, tap filled drinking water etc. and that also by the so called big organizations, may be unknowingly/ mistakingly; moreover these companies and the shareholders are making huge money; and the poor customer is verbally given the crown of the king at the end of the day. By the way, you have to do this to acquire the leader's status by selling your product/philosophy anyhow and SM suggests you to declare the customer king or God or likewise in an extremely shrewd manner. While the fact is, you can properly understand your customer and deliver them satisfactorily only if you consider the customer behaving as a prostitute as discussed in the earlier shrewd strategies. The moment you understand the matter in this manner, half of your strategies are developed. The point to be noted is that you should not openly address your customer that way. It is for internal use. Use of the term King and God is perfect when customers have gathered to listen to you on certain occasions; call them King, God etc., they will go home happily.

Whenever you do well in the market and you earn good profits, inform it to the public that it is due to the faith of the customers that has helped you do well in the market. This is again the right time to declare the customer as an emperor. For example there are many countries where there have been almost negligible presence of private insurers. When a private insurer enters into such countries, it starts building reputation and developing tryst by admitting it cleverly that people of this country seem to have good faith in private insurers and they have recognized the importance of quality advice and that of a superior approach to customer service. This has such an effect on the people that they really start thinking in this manner. This kind of PR exercise followed by other marketing activities in a coordinated manner really helps an organization in a fantastic beginning.

26. REDUCING NON-CORE OPERATIONS (IF TECHNOLOGY DOES NOT CHANGE FREQUENTLY, MANUFACTURE YOURSELF; IF IT CHANGES FREQUENTLY, GET IT OUTSOURCED)

A large organization time to time keeps on reducing operations in non-core areas. It can either be outsourced or can be manufactured through own resources. It has been observed that a time of large production comes when it is felt that it is better to produce on its own than to outsource. Again a period comes when it is felt beneficial to outsource than to manufacture itself. The elementary concept behind this is that if technology does not change frequently, manufacture yourself and if it changes frequently, get it outsourced; the whole burden and responsibility in the latter case will be of the external agents. One more option is widely used these days – the operations in the non-core areas are transformed into separate business units who can look out for the business from other sources also.

27. EMPHASIZING MARKET SHARE OVER MARGINS

Today most of the companies are concentrating on market share over margins, which is bound to intensify the competition. It is done through focusing on volumes, aggressive strategies and by restructuring and restrengthening of distribution network. Firstly,a company develops a framework to enhance the level of production. Then the aggressive marketing strategies are devised related to price and both pull and push demand. The quality of the product has to be according to the market standard in the initial stage, although in later stages, leaders can go well with an ordinary quality in spite of availability of better quality products by small players. And finally, the distribution network has to be restructured and it needs to be strengthened to meet the increased supply and demand aspects. This is a popular strategy among fast moving consumer goods companies. Even a small player can expand its operations and earnings in this manner.

28. ADOPTING PUSH ROUTE THROUGH NETWORK MARKETING INSTEAD OF PULL ROUTE THROUGH HEAVY ADVERTISEMENTS AT TIMES (THE WONDERS OF ISLAND EFFECT)

When in an excessively competitive market, a product is not fetching desired growth through the traditional dealer network, direct selling strategy proves to be a significant marketing tool and it can be seen being extensively used by different fmcg companies worldwide. It is normally materialized through network marketing. Numerous direct selling agents are appointed throughout the country and they are firstly asked to use the product themselves and then they are asked to appoint other members of the network under them who have to further use the product themselves and then to appoint members under them and so on.

One of it's most frequently used implementation methods being currently practiced by the companies these days is to call the customers for a meeting and then showing them big dreams like—you can have your island, personal Aero plane etc., if you become member of our network; adding more say, actually everybody wants to have it but just by doing a general job, these things can not be possessed; similarly in business also it is difficult to compete and survive these days, but if you join our network you can have all these dreams fulfilled and that also by giving just one third of the time you are working for your current job or that of the time you are spending in your business.

Then these fellows are interacted with six or seven old members uniformly scattered among the audience. These old members stand up one by one and again start saying the same thing in different style like—"I was not doing well in my job /business, I had a number of problems, then I came to know about this network marketing and you believe me, that changed my life totally. I did not work very hard for this but today I have my own bungalow, many big cars and a handsome bank balance. " All the old members confer exactly the same thing but their ways are different.

The psychological reason behind this is that when an ordinary person sees a number of rich persons in the splendor of good hotels, a strong desire emanates in his mind, a desire to be rich. And a good marketer always encashes this desire. That person is immediately registered as your member by taking some charges fixed by you. And now that he has paid some money to you, he wants to get it back with some profits; he starts efforts for making other members and the process goes on. A member of your network gives you dual benefit by acting as a customer as well as a salesman.

Well established brands working through traditional routes can use this strategy as a tool for accelerating the growth while the new organizations can save a lot on advertisement expenditures by going through this route. Remember that the companies /persons who start it, definitely make money if they have planned well but the network members have their own destinies. They get the share on the businesses coming up to the company due to them or due to the members appointed by them. The main idea is that the Island effect has such an impact on the common people that makes them behave as loyal customers as well as hard working salesmen.

29. HUMAN RESOURCES OUTSOURCING MANAGEMENT

Today one of the most exploiting, but highly profitable techniques, successfully used by a number of MNCs in different industries in different countries is human resource outsourcing. Now companies are becoming more and more attentive of their areas of competencies; they are least interested in taking up employees on their own payroll. There are many human resource provider firms operating globally. These HR firms provide manpower to the different companies and their respective HR firms remunerate these employees. The employees are recruited by the HR firms normally on contract basis. The profits of the HR firm and interest of the clients are given more importance than the future of these contract laborers. The job can either be for the project duration or for longer period depending upon the nature of work being outsourced. Normally it is used for the lower level jobs, while sometimes it has been seen being used for middle level jobs also. But you have to be very careful of these employees who are working for you but they are not on your payroll. They represent your company in the marketplace, so your goodwill is always at stake that makes it necessary for you to have vigilance over them.

This kind of outsourcing has actually arisen as a result of excess supply of skilled / non-skilled labor. Any company hardly thinks of their growth, promotions etc. When they gain experience at your workplace and complete the contract period, they themselves start looking for other jobs or they look forward for the renewal of the existing contract at your organization only. If they have performed well during the contract period, they can be even taken on your payroll. It is showing good results to many organizations that are using this strategy. But if they did not perform well during the contract period, they are not taken again. New ones are tried because this strategy is practiced normally when supply is more than enough.

The outsourced human resource can not create much problems to you as they are not in a position of exercising any right at your company; they have no choice but to go to even crime or terrorist affected areas on your instructions for the marketing or other related activities. The fact is that they simply would do any work assigned to them without leaving any scope for any resistance as long as they want to be on the job.

30. MAINTAINING THE POSITION OF DOMINANCE AND LEADERSHIP

Whenever a company from any industry holds a dominating position in the market, it becomes extremely important to take proper steps so as to maintain the dominant status in an era of hyper competition from small or big rivals. The necessary steps should be taken on continuous basis which may vary from industry to industry. For example today fmcg companies who are enjoying leadership status have to face tough competition from regional companies as well as from the MNCs. To retain their position they are rationalizing prices of different brands; secondly new variants of brands are regularly being introduced; they are upgrading the trade and promotional schemes continuously; they are going for a better advertisement strategy every next time; and making efforts to reduce cost of production by every possible improvement measure the company can undertake. That is how the leaders maintain, contain and retain the leadership position.

31. DIRECTLY TARGETING THE TARGET MARKETS

Competition is rising day by day. The marketing activities have also been getting smarter with the passage of time and simultaneously the costs of marketing has also increased substantially. Consultancy costs, advertisement costs etc. have increased so much that companies are always looking at better options at reasonable cost. A very good technique used by certain top notch companies is targeting the target markets directly as part of their marketing activities. This strategy is widely used by soft drinks industry, satellite channels, cellular service providers etc. Companies from these industries are using very simple methods of getting connected with youth related events like college festivals, concerts, roadshows and likewise. This gives an opportunity to the companies to develop a strong relationship with its customers directly, which has a long lasting impact. Various events like music competitions, fashion shows etc. are organized by these companies to achieve the main purpose of establishing an enduring relationship with the customers. There are certain financial institutions of world fame that have been going for this practice for a long time. Their sales people approach to a certain group of people only, decided by the company as target customers. They meet these selected persons and try to sell the financial products to them directly. This strategy therefore can not be termed nascent as it has been in use successfully for a very long time.

32. SUSTAINED EFFORTS FOR COMPETING WITH RIVALS IN COST CUTTING

Due to rising costs of raw materials in almost every industry, the cost of production is increasing day by day. But it is not possible to increase the price of the goods so frequently and proportionately because regular price variations could lead to disastrous results for the normal products. Exceptions to this rule are the scarce products. Every player eyes at cost cutting in the best possible way which actually is a continuous process. The leading firms from every industry compete and fight with rivals not only in terms of product quality, features, advertisements strategies etc. but also in terms of cost cutting. There are different strategies available for cost cutting, which is normally initiated by downsizing the work force after studying the pros and cons properly. The second strategy is to eliminate some products who have not yielded expected results even after much efforts or who are getting badly affected by internal or external or both factors. But this strategy should be used with much conscience as there is a possibility that some products may be stopped to be produced which can actually be profitable in near future according to the market perception and as per forecasting by the business experts. All these aspects should be studied and analyzed properly by having a clear watch over emerging markets and marketing trends throughout the world. Never let your competitor go ahead of you in terms of genuine and logical cost cutting.

33. INCREASING PRICE WITHOUT NEGATIVE EFFECTS

There are times when it becomes imperative for the manufacturer to increase the price due to many reasons in the highly competitive markets. To do so, the leading companies go for different Shrewd Marketing strategies, which can be very easily felt and observed in normal life. Those shrewd strategies are as such—

A. Increase the Price with a Small Gift; After the Stock is Over, Stop the Gift and Let the Increased Price Stay—

Most of the fast moving consumer goods companies are following the strategy of increasing the price, giving a small gift free with the product and when the stock is exhausted from the market, the products are sold at new increased price and the gift is stopped. This is how they cleverly make a rise in the prices of their products. This strategy can be used in other industries as well, where if it is not possible to give a free gift with the product, then price can be increased by adding some features whose costs are lesser than the actual increase in price. This is practiced every now and then in automobile and durables industries.

B. Reduce the Quantity of the Product at the Earlier Marked Price—

If a soap weighing 200 units was sold at a price, say x, then instead of making an increase in the price x, the quantity can be reduced from 200 units to 190 units or likewise some changes can be made depending upon the magnitude of the intended increase in the price. This practice can be successfully exercised by co-ordinating it properly with new trade schemes and better advertisement strategies. e. g. Repositioning the product in terms of improved looks or changed features which has actually been done without making any extra expenditure.

C. Degrade Cleverly the Quality of the Product—A Happy Time to Encash Your Brand Image—

Now that you have worked reasonably well in the market for a good amount of time, your brand image helps you in getting rid of the pressure of increasing the price. Customers are happy with your brand and little deviation from the quality would not let them understand about the quality compromise. eg. Can a customer identify a little change (actually deterioration) in the quality of his regular soap subject to the maintained fragrance and looks exactly as it was before. Similarly in durables industry, some parts are replaced with cheaper ones (but obviously not with extremely bad ones), metallic parts getting replaced with cheaper plastic parts etc. are the commonly used techniques in these industries. The quality degradation should not be allowed to be understood by the customers – it should be managed that way. This strategy would differ from industry to industry in terms of magnitude and the ways in which quality could be compromised without a clear and visible effect. This is a rational way to react in the markets experiencing a need to increase the prices of certain products.

34. GO ON INVESTING IN THE COUNTRIES WHICH ARE INEFFICIENT, BUT ARE ABLE TO PROVIDE YOU FAVORABLE BUSINESS AND MANUFACTURING CONDITIONS

Having a global outlook, always eye on the

nations who are inefficient in terms of optimum utilization of their resources of every kind. There are many developing nations of the world who are trying very hard to attract foreign investors. They are ready to provide you all favorable business conditions like different type of rebates and exemptions, hassle free permissions, excellent infrastructure, good law and order conditions etc. It has been experienced that the developing nations are not able to provide these conditions to the indigenous manufacturers; while they are always eager to provide all these things to the foreign investors. So never fail to take advantage of this behavior of the developing countries. Their inefficiency leaves behind lots of opportunity for you to do well at their place. Just try to recognize the opportunities that can be explored by you for your optimum advantage. Like a large population cannot be cared and nurtured properly by the local government of a developing nation, while this large population caters you in terms of extremely cheap manpower that ultimately enables you to go for labor intensive techniques of production in those nations. Same fundamental applies to other resources also.

35. SHREWD MANAGEMENT FOR EMPLOYEE'S CONTROL

Successful companies keep on motivating their employees at every level. They try to create an impression in the market (without letting the people know that they are deliberately doing so) that they are the companies that have high moral values and who strictly follow ethical principles and whose employees are considered to be the assets of the organization. They keep on sending these messages time to time by organizing certain activities in the internal as well as external environment that is ultimately aimed at fetching immense respect to their employees from the competitors, by the channel partners, and by other employees of their own organization. Now once this reputation is created, a number of tasks become extremely easy for these employees at various occasions. e. g. If you are a marketer from a leading durables company with a good brand image and you wish to change your trade partner in a particular territory, you get offers coming up from different parties in the business the moment you expressed your wish to have a new trade partner.

But at the same time it is the responsibility of the board members to keep close vigilance on the activities of the people at top level. Similarly, senior marketing people also must have attention over the activities of the staff working at lower levels. Remember, if any member of your result oriented marketing team leaves your organization during your business seasons or, your strategies are revealed by a top level manager who is leaving, can badly affect your business figure for the particular month or for even the quarter. Your board of directors has to be so attentive that every activity of the top-level employees in and out of the office that could affect the business should be watched immediately and sensibly without disturbing their personal lives and without creating much chaos. We all have seen the instances that people at top level have been removed from the companies on several occasions in spite of their having worked extremely well. It is simply due to the smelling of something wrong being planned or being even thought by these people. Remember, even your CEO also needs more salary, more perks and a bigger status, which can easily be provided by some of your competitors. But they will select this man only when he reveals all your soft, hard and shrewd strategies. Although it is very difficult to stop this man from doing so but, you can at least be prepared to protect yourself from the disturbances that might arise due to these kind of unwanted happenings.

See, a marketing head can introduce many variants of products; he can go for massive advertisement expenditure; or he can totally introduce a new distribution system and then suddenly he leaves—how troublesome it would be for you? Can you imagine? It is therefore strongly recommended to have an ability to sense every small and big things inside your organization. Shrewd Marketing suggests you to go for predictions based precautions that ultimately should be based on shrewd thinking.

Shrewd Marketing Level III

36. CONCENTRATE MORE ON THE ADVERTISEMENTS OF THE DRUGS MEANT FOR DEADLY DISEASES, RATHER THAN ON PREVENTION TECHNIQUES

All the industries aim at having more and more customers for a sustainable growth over a long period of time. But for the pharmaceutical companies, in normal cases, more customers mean more people having diseases. Although Shrewd Marketing is against of unethical issues, but here it is necessary to reveal the above fact because marketing strategies of these companies are developed by keeping this hard fact in the mind. Companies manufacturing drugs for dreaded diseases like hepatitis, Breast cancer etc. are rarely found to be focusing more on prevention of these diseases. If they develop preventive vaccines, they advertise it in a way that gives a feel to the customer that these companies want the nation disease free and that is why they should buy and use it as a matter of prevention. While actually it is a vaccine selling strategy. In certain cases where vaccines have not been developed, but drugs are available – these drugs are advertised and not the measures to prevent the disease. If the prevention measures are given some importance, then that is given with the medicine and kept in the carton, which is actually printed on a paper & folded many times that hardly attracts someone's attention. Afterall these companies are also doing business, and still the sole motive of business is to make profits ;other motives are simply the strategies to promote business. This is very easy to find the strategy of concentrating more on the advertisements of drugs meant to cure deadly diseases, instead of recommending the prevention through a better communication process. Normally the advertisement text does not appear like this—"you can prevent breast cancer by taking following precautions......... . ". Instead it appears like this—"Now our drugs are available for breast cancer at every medical store; get in on your Doctor's prescription; we are a company engaged in fighting with this disease for past certain number of years..............".

It is a very sophisticated strategy, so it can be felt being used very carefully with utmost shrewdness.

37. SBS (SOCIAL BACTERIA STRATEGY)—SHOW HAVING EXTRA RESPONSIBILITIES OF SOCIAL DEVELOPMENT, CUSTOMER DELIGHTMENT ETC.

The fashion of the day, the need of the day, the

strategy of the day is—SBS (Social Bacteria Strategy). Under this strategy every leading organization in almost every industry shows necessarily to have certain social responsibilities. It is presented in the society so well that it always seems to be a reality. While this is a strategy to appeal the masses through behavioral route; people think that this company really understands its duties towards the society; and this thinking of the customers accrues some privilege to the company during the buying process of the customers. Just for gaining this advantage, every big organization claims to have certain social responsibilities. In business, every penny is supposed to yield some returns and that is why this Social Bacteria Strategy is practiced in co-ordination with the well planned business strategies. e. g. If a company is going to invest heavily in a new country, it donates some money for AIDS or likewise for any other social cause before it actually makes the investment; it contributes some percentage of the price of a product to non governmental organizations engaged in some social cause (although you spend more on advertising about the contribution than the contribution itself) etc. —these are some of the popular and well known examples of the Social Bacteria Strategy being practiced off late. A social activist can not be a good marketer; but the marketer who is an excellent practitioner of SBS will fetch maximum benefits to a firm through a pragmatic approach. To be a practitioner of this shrewd strategy you do not have to actually spend time on social activities; you just have to focus on deciding and funding your social responsibility at minimum cost with maximum returns.

It is simply contemplated that how an organization can impress it's target customers differently & to a great extent by doing good for the poors, the diseased or the deprived ones and, then the SBS is evolved.

Secondly you should never miss an opportunity to say that you just don't want to satisfy your customers, but you want to delight them. Apart from trying to be marginally better than the competitors in terms of quality and service, you don't have to do anything else than to keep on saying that – " we want to delight our customers". It is because you are already delivering as per the market expectations; what you need is to present it well to your target customers by seeking their attention towards your brand and then letting them know about the improved features of your product, which you are offering to delight them.

38. NEVER MISS TO COPE UP WITH MARKET CHANGES

The market always keeps on changing in terms of tastes and preferences, fashion, product renovations/modifications etc. The change can occur either from the customer front or from the competitor's front. An intelligent firm always tries to meet the improved expectations of the customers and to compete with the innovative techniques being applied by the competitors in making some improvements in the product. The moment you lag behind in offering the product as per latest trends, you will start facing the problem of decreased sales volume, customer's losing interest in your products and your survival will be at stake. So you must plan in a way that would enable you to have a flexibility to make changes in technology, changes in marketing strategies etc. in the excessive volatile markets. You must be ready all the time to go for a change as per the market demand.

39. ANNOUNCING REWARDS FOR SACKING EMPLOYEES, WHEN YOU WANT TO DOWNSIZE

There are times when organizations face a situation of ensuring that they cater to the ever rising needs of the business. Secondly,it is felt extremely important to position the company for long term success through cost effectiveness which is possible only through the process of continuous cost cutting. As a measure of cost cutting the most important step being taken by many multi national corporations is downsizing. The best practice to achieve the target of pink slips is to announce internally an incentive on each employee being sacked to the top executives. This strategy is quite often seen being used by many organizations but it is implemented secretly/silently to avoid the resistance and in normal cases people come to know about it after it is successfully implemented.

40. DEVELOPING VIRUSES (DISTURBING ELEMENTS) FOR COMPETITORS, WITHOUT GETTING NOTICED

The fundamental of sales confers that for selling an anti virus there has to be a virus, does not matter who develops it. In IT industry, developing viruses is a common phenomenon that keeps on disturbing the leaders and of course the small companies also. Manyatimes it so happens that as a competitive move your research and development department develops a virus for your competitors. Your competitors are affected by this virus and the news spreads in the industry sending a message that your competitors can be easily disturbed by these kind of suddenly emanated viruses that ultimately maligns their reputation. One has to develop the disturbing elements for the competitors in whichever industry one is. Remember that leaders have to do it time to time and similarly they have to face it also time to time. In soft drinks industry, the practice of buying competitor's empty bottles and breaking them for the purpose of creating scarcity of competitor's soft drinks in the market, is not unknown to any aware marketer. If it is done during seasons, it badly affects the supply of rival's products. If in the confectionary industry, some pieces of glass is found in a chocolate of a reputed company, it can be a malpractice performed by a competitor. Therefore, you have to face it in the industry and to give it a defeat, you may also have to go for similar strategies if you want to remain in business. The leaders use this strategy to kill the small players and to harm badly the strong competitors. Normally when it is used against the leaders, it does not create much impact because they have their own shrewd team working actively in the market. They can even take it positively in their own favour by terming it a malpractice carried out by some of its competitors or by some anti social elements whose probe is going on. They can use these gimmicks even in genuine cases of adulteration in their products.

This strategy is to be used with utmost care and secretly. You can not afford being caught while using this strategy against some competitor. In soft drinks industry, trade partners and restaurants etc. are bribed for not selling the competitor's products. These channel partners can be offered certain additional commission on the total sales at the end of every financial year.

41. BEYOND SALESMANSHIP – APPLYING TEAM EFFORT IN SELLING

A time was there when selling was important from the point of view that marketers had to sell and they had to generate revenue. So strategies were developed so as to sell the products through different means, particularly through salesmanship. Now the market has become smarter. Your whole marketing team will have to work in unity with the sole purpose of selling that ensures repeat sales. This ensuring of repeat sales requires much more effort than simply selling. Actually from the starting of the buying process to ultimate consumption, a customer can pass through different experiences. You just have to identify these experiences at different levels and formulate the strategies to emerge as a winner at every level of customer's experience so as to ensure repeat sales. Every person engaged in different marketing functions will have to bear the fact in his mind and he will have to make it sure that his action and services had no faults, instead they were so good that a customer will definitely like to get this experience again. If every marketing professional ensures this, your job is well done. You have to start convincing your customer with a cleverly made advertisement followed by good sales promotional schemes, proper merchandising, the retailer's interest in selling your product that assures you competitive advantage at the last point also and, a very good after sales service. A commendable approach by some traditional marketers is to perceive every customer as the only customer of an organization. Supposing this, your whole marketing efforts should focus on satisfying this customer. Same level of focus is tried to be given to every customer for ensuring customer delightment as a whole.

42. NEVER OFFER THE BEST QUALITY WHEN YOU ARE EYING AT GLOBAL MARKETS—OFFER THE STANDARD THE CUSTOMER IS HABITUATED OF USING, A LITTLE BETTER THAN THE CURRENT STANDARD WOULD BE EXCELLENT FOR THAT COUNTRY

Whenever you are eying at entering into global markets, you need to develop the product strategy in a very careful manner. Suppose you are from a developed nation where products of very high quality are sold and consumed and you want your operations to be expanded to developing nations. At this point you will have to study the quality of product being offered by different companies in this new country for you. You will find that the quality of your current product is far superior than the quality of this country's products. In this situation, you will have to produce the product which has better quality than the standard of this country but it is inferior than your original quality. This kind of operation is normally started in many ways like —either by making a joint venture with the companies engaged in production of similar products or by acquisitions or by starting your own manufacturing unit in that country which will definitely use a poor technology but nevertheless it will be better than the technological standard of this developing country but not as good as your parent country's standards.

Shrewd Marketing Level IV

43. BE EXTREMELY CAREFUL IN NAMING AN INDUSTRY – WHY BUSINESS PROCESS OUTSOURCING WHEN IT COULD HAVE BEEN BUSINESS PROCESS SOURCING (BPS INSTEAD OF BPO)

Talking about Information Technology, having the chunk of talent coming up to join the industry of applying brain and getting more money immediately. In recent times Business Process Outsourcing has emerged as a cost cutting tool for several big and small companies throughout the world. These days a USA or UK based company opting for the BPO route, manages to get the queries and problems of its customers solved by the people working for them in far flung countries like India, Philippines etc. These people are trained in a way that they can easily handle the queries coming up from abroad. Technical know-how, language and accent etc. are taught to these people. It has really worked well for many companies off late in terms of cost reduction. Quality manpower in the developing nations is available at such a cheaper rate that is really amazing when you compare it with the wages at the USA and UK or other developed countries. So taking advantage of this is of huge importance in an era of hyper competition. But Business Process outsourcing industry has been witnessing lots of resistance from the people and political parties of the affected nations from where these jobs moved out and finally got done in developing nations. It is simply due to the wrong naming of this industry which is – Business Process Outsourcing (BPO). This industry could better have been named as Business Process Sourcing (BPS). The term "Outsourcing" has such a psychological impact on the minds of the people that they perceive it as the main reason for the jobs of their country moving out to other countries. This term "Outsourcing" further means to these people that they are the source and people abroad are outsource. While it is fundamental rule of the business that resources in any form should be made available from where it costs minimum to the company and in the era of globalization the businesses understand no boundaries; in this case if companies are finding it economical to get the work done in less developed countries through the local people there at cheaper rates, then how can it be seen as a problem. It has been creating lots of chaos off late. Had it been called Business Process Sourcing, there would have been much less trouble. It is therefore strongly recommended that when a business is going to be innovated or when a business is newly coming up in shape, it should be named carefully.

44. INSTITUTIONAL SALES IN RIVAL'S ESTABLISHED MARKETS — PROBE ABOUT THE MICRO DETAILS OF THE COMPETITOR'S PRODUCT, FIND A SALEABLE DEFECT AND ATTACK ON THIS

Institutional sales always draw attention of the marketers as an important area to increase the sales, which can be possible only through excellent performance of sales people through extraordinary knack. Here, your marketing personnel approach to different organizations for the consumption of your product at their place. Either your sales people fix up the deal or they don't. It is okay if they fix it up; but if they are not able to establish a sales deal at a particular institution because some competitor of yours had already finalized the deal and they are the regular supplier of that product to this organization, it is tried to break up the competitor's relations with this institution so that you get the opportunity to serve. The shrewd marketing suggests you in this situation to go for some Research and Development (R&D) work. You take the product of your competitor who is the current supplier of a particular product to an institution; get it tested and checked on a number of factors till you get some defect that can be saleable for you, which means that you can claim in the market that this product is having such and such defects. For example, suppose you are a player in the packed drinking water industry; and from a particular Airlines you are not getting business because some competitor of yours is already having a business relationship with them and it is supplying drinking water regularly without compromising on quality, timeliness etc. In this situation, you should take the drinking water of this market player and let it pass through a series of tests like – E-Coli, Coliform or through other contamination tests likewise. Normally a company Keeps on testing it on different type of contaminations till some thing wrong is detected in the competitor's product. One practicing this strategy should silently test one's product also on this scale and if this too is at fault, then again silently this defect is rectified from the product and then much hue and cry is created about the competitor's product. Simultaneously the Airlines as well as the media are informed about this defect persisting in the competitor's product. The particular Airlines will be in a perplexed situation with full of fear about it's passenger's health; and it might look for an alternative at this point of time that requires your marketing team to act and follow up aggressively. Your chances of getting the business are very high now notwithstanding the fact that competitor will also leave no stone unturned for controlling this situation of unexpected emergency. But one should never miss to remove this defect from one's own product; in case the defect was there in your product also and you rectified it but your stock is still available in the market, you should then wait for some time and this strategy should not be used until and unless your whole current stock is fully exhausted from the market. In some cases, government agencies will also criticize these objectionable products being offered to the passengers. Every now and then you hear about some or other bacteria in eatables or in beverages. This strategy has a heavy and short term impact, so you will have to be very fast in acquiring your rival's clients. The strategy seeks much careful and clever approach.

45. CONFRONTATION OF RIVAL'S PRODUCTS THROUGH THIRD PARTY

Nowadays in many industries, a different strategy is used to prove the fact that the competitor's product is not up to the mark. Those customers who have had bad experiences in using your rival's products are highlighted and brought to the attention of the pubic. Although it can be difficult to find out such people, but it is not impossible. Moreover you can deliberately make anyone telling and discussing about the unpleasant experience that he went through while using your rival's products. In your advertisement campaign, these kind of persons should be shown saying clearly that they had had difficulty in using a particular company's product; or they can say that according to their experiences, other products in this range also did not give them total satisfaction, while when they used your product they felt totally satisfied and that is why they recommend other customers also to go for your product so that they don't have to face the same situation.

When you directly make your advertisements depict a message that using your products would give a customer maximum /total satisfaction—it may not appeal to the customers. But when you make customers say about their bad experiences with other brands in this range, and if simultaneously they say about a nice experience and good amount of satisfaction with your products; this really creates convincing impact on the minds of other customers to a great extent in your favor.

46. NEVER BE COMPLACENT IN BUSINESS

At the top management level of an organization you always keep one aspect in your mind that you don't have to be complacent in terms of performance in any department or at any profit centre or in any strategic business unit. Always set a target for every profit centre, which is if achieved, should not accrue a sense of satisfaction that might lead you in having a loose performance in the next quarter. The moment your people achieve the targets, give them a pat on the back and increase the target for the next quarter. This is how an organization keeps on increasing its turnover with passage of time which is mainly due to lack of complacency and due to continuous efforts for a sustainable growth. If you feel having reached to the saturation point in any industry where further growth is not pragmatically feasible, then go for expansions in related or non-related industries. The selection of industry should be based more on Return on Investment (ROI) and related aspects. Entering into entirely new industries is not perceived as a limitation nowadays.

47. GO EXPERIMENTAL TIME TO TIME IN A SMART WAY

One of the most important features of the successful organizations is to go experimental time to time in a smart way. They already have executed other strategic and marketing efforts skillfully for the achievement of the organizational goal. In addition to this they keep on performing certain highly creative acts on an experimental basis that is not very common to the industry in discussion. Like an organization can think of connecting the rural markets with Internet services by providing the technology and technical know-how to a few selected members of the community. And these members are handed over the responsibility of letting the company know about the requirements of different products in that particular area. Thus the company gets the dual benefit – sales enhancement in rural markets fetching more profits, secondly implications of Social Bacteria Strategy bringing huge respect and affection to the company.

An organization willing to establish customer loyalty in an experimental way started distributing bananas in the morning to the customers free of cost. In both the above examples the efforts have been found to be accruing wonders for the respective companies. You need to identify the creative ways of doing new things in the markets is the main idea behind this strategy.

48. THINK AND ACT BEYOND UNIQUE SELLING PROPOSITION (USP) AND UNIQUE MARKETING PROPOSITION (UMP); DEVELOP A SHREWD MARKETING TEAM (SMT) BY SELECTING THE BEST PERFORMERS OF YOUR ORGANIZATION FOR OPTIMUM MARKETING RESULTS

There was a time when organizations used to depend greatly on Unique Selling Proposition of a product, which later on got broadly promoted to Unique Marketing Proposition. In the current scenario of tough competition, where every uniqueness is bound to be copied without making any delay; the companies are looking at better strategic marketing tools. For this purpose, you always need to develop a Shrewd Marketing Team (SMT) inside your organization. This SMT will comprise of intelligent members from different levels of the organization. Every member of SMT has to necessarily be a proved great market performer. The size and function of the team should depend on the size of the organization, nature of the market, market practices adopted by the competitors etc. It is not necessary to appoint the SMT separately; you can always select some of your top performers from across the country or from across the globe to carry out the responsibility of SMT. The Shrewd Marketing Team of an organization need to identify the global and local shrewd marketing practices and, depending upon this, they have to suggest and develop strategies for every area of marketing, like suggesting desirable features and uniqueness of product variants, creating channel partner's penchant towards one's product, ascertaining the need of advertising differently, formulating extraordinary ways to attract masses and likewise.

If you carry out these functions by forming a formal or informal SMT, your marketing activities will always fetch the results in the expected proportions. The SMT leaves no marketing gimmicks by your rivals unattacked and unanswered, thus trying to ascertain your dominance over global and regional competitors.

49. LEADERS ALWAYS GO FOR TOTAL MARKETING EFFORT (TME)

Total Marketing Effort (TME) is the backbone of an organization's success. Every member of an organization is a marketer in some or other sense. A customer can pass through different people of an organization before/during/after the product's/service's whole consumption / utilization period. Like a customer buying your product say in the durables industry can initially meet the sales people or/and the retailer (channel partner), then service staff etc. A customer has certain expectations from all these people. Then supposing that he got certain problems related to the product that could not be solved by the local service centre, he needs to go through some requests to the branch offices of the company. There again he gets his queries and problems solved by some people. Now you see that how many people did he meet during the uses of the product. If at any level he does not get the satisfaction or gets some irritation, he might not go for your brand again or he might not suggest it to others. Because at this point you are found to be weak, and the Shrewd Marketing Team (SMT) of other companies will quickly identify it and ultimately you will be attacked heavily by your competitors. Remember, as you are attacking on other's weaknesses, others are also trying to find an opportunity to attack you. Therefore it is suggested to train your employees and channel members in a way that they all satisfy the clients at the moment they come across. Every employee of your organization is your Brand ambassador and so they all have to work by keeping in mind that even if they are not directly involved in the marketing activities, their role is inseparable from the Total Marketing Effort being undertaken by the organization whose sole aim is to make profits which is possible only when customers are satisfied at every point.

50. ALWAYS DISCLOSE THE MARKETING STRATEGIES AND FUTURE EXPECTATIONS WITHIN YOUR OWN ORGANIZATION

This is in the quintessential nature of a good organization to disclose the marketing strategies and the level of future performance expected from the workforce. When the marketing people at every level are well acquainted of the marketing strategies being implemented at the top level, it gives them an insight to coordinate their activities in accordance with the organization's desired level of performance. At this stage both their future actions and future thinking should match with the organizational strategic pattern. At the same time, the expected level and extent of performance should also be made very much clear. For a high degree of performance, employees work harder; while in the organizations where future performance is not made precisely known, employees work with laxity. An organization should strictly communicate the expectations from the marketing staffs in the current as well as in the next quarters and for achieving it pragmatically, the set of marketing strategies should be clearly explained to them. Although there are some instances where it is not preferred to reveal all the marketing strategies to everyone.

51. FOCUS YOURSELF AS A COMPANY THAT ALWAYS MAINTAINS A HIGH QUALITY STANDARD; DOES NOT MATTER WHETHER YOU FULFILL SUCH CLAIM OR NOT

Most of the customer oriented companies have a tendency to focus themselves as a company that maintains a high quality standard for the delightment of their customers. It helps them in positioning their brands as strong brands with the image of a company offering products of fine quality. You definitely have to maintain a reasonable quality standard in your products, which should not give any bad or negative message regarding the quality aspects to the customers. It is not always necessary for you to possess the best quality only. Simply maintain the reasonable quality level and buttress it with shrewd marketing artifices. For example a toothpaste manufacturing company claims that its products are certified by some national or international dental agencies/associations. It is a fact that very few customers care about the existence/non existence and other details of these certifying organizations. But an ordinary customer surely receives the message that the products of this company are certified by different dental organizations, so these products must be of superior quality. That is how a smart company tries to focus in the market regarding the high quality standard in it's offerings.

52. ENSURE THAT YOUR PRODUCT DESERVES THE PRICE YOU ARE CHARGING FROM THE CUSTOMERS

Always try to present your products in a way that conveys a message to the society that the product's price justifiably matches to the quality and features of the product. Keep on communicating to the market that profit is not the sole objective of your firm. You want to delight your customers by offering the best at minimum price. And that is why you are charging this much. It is to be noticed carefully that although you have big spends on quality maintenance, on research and development, on timely product delivery and on ascertainment of its smooth availability in the market etc. , but you are consistently declaring that you want to charge minimum for the product as you are a customer oriented company. Once you continue this practice for sometime, it gets established in the minds of the customers that your products really deserve the price you are charging for them. Whenever a customer buys a product, he must not feel getting cheated in terms of price. For example there are several markets in different cities throughout the globe where bargaining is done. At these places sellers initially ask for a foolishly inflated price, that immediately gives a feel to the customer that he is being cheated and he never feels satisfaction with whatever price he had to pay finally after the bargaining. A brand can not be well positioned that way. When you want to establish in the market with a long term perspective, you should always try to justify your product by properly matching its features and quality with the price you are asking for.

53. ENCASH THE HUMAN PSYCHOLOGY DEFECTS OF REACTING SERIOUSLY ON NEGATIVE ASPECTS INSTEAD OF ACTING MORE SENSIBLY ON THE POSITIVE FEATURES OF A PRODUCT

The human psychology has certain reactive patterns, according to which it has been experienced by the marketers that if you keep on emphasizing over the negative aspects/ features of your competitors products, it leaves a long lasting impression on the minds of the customers. Like in your advertisement for a car you can write that following companies are not providing certain features in their cars by giving the name of the companies and the features they are deliberately not offering in a particular country. The moment customers hear about these companies, the negative features start coming to their mind. It is therefore seen that companies always keep on trying to find out the shortcomings/defects in the rival's products and then these shortcomings are highlighted. While you want your customers to be associated with you for whole life, so your brand provides all these features. This presentation has such an impact on the customers that whenever a customer wants to buy a product, he gives a negative evaluation to the products of such companies and a positive and favorable evaluation to your products, thus giving you a chance to prove yourself. This is a commonly and extensively used practice in durables and automobile sector. Although almost every industry is using this strategy in some or other way through the sales people or through the channel partners.

Thus it is very important to learn to earn benefits from the customer's psychology of acting more seriously on negative features rather than that on positive features of a product. This sophisticated method has to be devised very carefully for your industry so as to have the best possible impact.

54. LEARN TO HANDLE AND CONTROL THE CUSTOMER BY MAKING VALUE ADDITIONS CONTINUOUSLY

You have to accept the fact that every good marketer is working very hard in the market. Some improved efforts are made by one, which is immediately followed and superceded by another. This induces a customer to behave inconsistently with different brands. Therefore you will have to be continuously changing and improving. Then you need to be uniquely customer driven where it is necessary to cope up with the market changes as per and if possible then beyond market expectations. To handle and to control today's customer, you have to make such value additions continuously, which ultimately has a capacity to cater the changing moods of the customer. You can not say at any point of time that now you are producing the best quality and no improvements are possible. Leaders always keep on thinking of making improvements in even their well performing products also. For example in IT industry, various software companies always try to bring in improved versions of the existing products /services, that can be easily seen in the markets.

55. ENSURE THAT YOUR BRAND IS ALWAYS GIVEN WEIGHTAGE WHEN A CUSTOMER IS TO BUY A PRODUCT IN THIS CATEGORY

Leaders always make it certain that their brands are definitely taken into consideration when a customer intends to buy a product in this category. They try to emerge as a winner on the every step of a customer's buying process – which starts right from need recognition to evaluation of alternatives to buying finally, followed by post purchase behavior. Although practically there can be many other possibilities in between the process explained above. You make efforts to establish your brand in such a way that whenever a customer feels a need to buy a product in certain category, your brand comes to his mind. Then when he is considering different alternatives, your brand shall get due weightage. It is all because you have positioned your brand in that way— either by regular publicity or by word of mouth or what have you of this. Then the customers will finally buy your product only.

56. YOU MUST ENSURE CUSTOMER'S AFFILIATION TOWARDS YOUR BRAND FOR YEARS

Whenever you are making public relations

exercises or going for advertisements, you should try to highlight the things in a way that sends a message to the society that you are going to stay for a long time and you possess long term plans in terms of continuous product development and product diversifications. This strategy can be materialized through creative publicity measures involving people of different generations, by having an attitude of perfection towards completeness of a product and by executing the marketing functions with a strong orientation towards customers. You can see leaders in different industries having developed a 10 or 20 or even 25 years plan with enough flexibility. It is more evident in IT and electronics industry. It gives the customer an opportunity to think in a way that this brand will always be catering them with best quality in the long run also. Due to this, you get an opportunity of emerging as a brand that was known by grand parents, further used by parents and still considered with respect by the new and younger generation. It is always suggested to devise different ways of ensuring customer's affiliation towards one's brand with a long term perspective.

57. TO THINK AS A GOOD MARKETER, LEARN TO THINK AS A CUSTOMER FIRST

While evolving marketing strategies for different levels of management it is obvious and excessively significant to contemplate over different marketing strategies being used by your rivals. This gives you a basis to evolve a better strategy.

But an equally important aspect to be seriously considered here is the customer's prerogative. How a customer thinks about a product; what does he expects from a product; why will he buy a product; and product of which brand will be bought by him, etc. Once all these points are noted down and, a serious thought is given on these factors and that on the rival's marketing strategies simultaneously, and then you finally come up with a strategic solution that concentrates on satisfying all these factors. These will place you at a position where you have so well conceived and strong marketing strategies that would help you significantly in ascertainment of your leadership position. It is therefore suggested to every good marketer to learn to think as a customer first and then to develop the strategies.

58. CUSTOMERS DON'T POSSESS VALUES IN TERMS OF LOYALTY TOWARDS A PARTICULAR BRAND, SO LEARN TO ACT ACCORDINGLY

It has been experienced that customers do not normally possess values in terms of staying with a certain brand for a long time. Today customer is very cautious, vigilant, choosy and more and more demanding. Consequently, the customer keeps on moving from one brand to another better brand as per their perceptions and understandings. To operate in this situation, you as a marketer also have to act in a clever way. Although it is very important according to the business ethics, but practically one can not every time afford values or the concept of rightness or wrongness in this difficult situation. So it becomes necessary for you to act wisely in such markets by applying different tricks through advertisements. While advertising for televisions, children are shown watching TV for a long time without any stress on the eyes due to use of superior technology. Now the marketer's perspective is that it will induce children into asking parents for buying this TV. But this kind of advertisement simultaneously induces children into spending more time on televisions, which is needed to be overlooked by a marketer.

One has to simply ascertain that how one's products are sold maximum and how one keeps on formulating ways to strengthen it's position in such a clever way that can never be understood by the customers. At this moment, it is recommended to look at the values aspects to a limited extent in designing the whole marketing programs. You can always find some big firms showing some misleading advertisements; or they can be seen fighting openly with rivals in the market; in IT industry it is every now and then heard that such and such company is always going for anti competitive practices etc. are all the examples of this.

59. CONTROL THE CLEVEREST CUSTOMER, THE ORDINARY ONES WILL AUTOMATICALLY COME UNDER YOUR CONTROL

Contemplate over one aspect that who can be the most clever customer for your product ; what will he expect from your brand ; how you can ascertain his total satisfaction; do you have the genuine qualities that would convince him into buying your product. Create as many questions as you can about this cleverest customer. Then find out the solution that where you are all right and where you are lacking. Whenever you feel some drawback or inefficiency in satisfying this customer—a need arises to properly identify and rectify the problems ; and you should continue this process till every shortcoming is removed. Now go through the same set of questions again and, now you will find that you are in a position where you can satisfy your most clever customer. A basic thing to be understood here is that you got so many requirements (here mentioned in terms of questions) because you considered all the expectations of a most clever and smart customer. The ordinary customers do not have so many expectations because they think ordinarily. So when your cleverest customer is happily buying your product, these ordinary customers will also be definitely buying it happily.

60. POSITION YOUR BRAND IN A WAY THAT BRINGS A SENSE OF FULFILLMENT AND PRIDE AMONG YOUR CUSTOMERS

You should try your brand to be positioned in such a manner that enhances the confidence level of your customers. Apart from the satisfaction from basic utility of the product, customers must gain a sense of pride while/ after buying/using your product is the main idea here. You can go for advertisements by using statements / punchlines like—image building brand; don't just have it, possess it; make others envy by using it; buy our product because we have been ranked No. 1 in our category by certain agencies; use this product because it is used by most of the beautiful movie stars of the world etc. —all these aspects aim at simply one thing i. e. to render customer a special feelings about the product. Most of the advertisement strategies of the leading and innovative companies are largely based on this philosophy.

61. ASCERTAIN THAT YOUR BRAND IS A SPECIAL ONE, THAT HAS UNIQUE FEELINGS ASSOCIATED WITH IT

A smart marketer always ensures that his brand has certain special emotions and sentiments attached with it. You might have seen the instances where greeting cards figuring lovely babies are sent to pregnant women; condoms of a particular brand can be distributed to newly married couples; then freebies are given to kids with meals at restaurants etc— these are all simply the ways to attach your customer emotionally with your brand and which are undoubtedly more than ordinary promotional measures. It can further be practiced by involving the customers in promotional activities time to time through different contests/ challenges or through other mega events etc. It really works wonders for you if you ensure that with every purchase, your customers get some sense of caring or affection. Keep on saying in the market that—we are a brand who cares for the customers.

62. FIVE STAGE BRAND STRATEGY

A product is used by customers of different age. A kid has different thinking, a mature person has gotten another approach and so on. A brand should be developed in a manner that the people from different demographic and geographical background get some affiliation with this particular brand. Leaders follow this strategy very regularly. Here it is important to understand that there are numerous products which are of use to a particular group or sex. For example kids have nothing to do with women's napkins. So in this case the strategy has to be essentially customized for the target market only. But in industries like fast moving consumer goods, mass oriented approach can be easily seen being practised. Even in car purchases, there are times when a customer's wife or kids play important role in making choices—in this case also branding strategy is developed by keeping all these groups in mind. You just have to find out the implications of this strategy to your industry.

Your branding strategies should always concentrate on positioning your brand in the minds of the young class of people. As the time passes, your brand name acquires a stable and permanent place in their minds.

The five-stage brand strategy suggests the brand development process in a manner that requires a marketer to concentrate on five classes of people. According to this strategy, a company's plans related to branding should have some focus on each of the following— 1. kids, 2. teenagers, 3. young people, 4. middle & old aged and, 5. main target group. Obviously, the most important of all these is to focus maximum on the main target group, but if you focus a little bit on other four classes also, it would help you in generating good demand for whatever you produce for whichever section of the society.

A new company adopting the five-stage brand strategy will have great potential and probabilities of emerging as a major brand as part of the long term strategy. And major brands can strengthen their existing position with this approach.

63. PUT YOUR COMPETITORS IN DIFFICULT SITUATIONS TIME TO TIME (BY SUDDENLY COMING UP WITH NEW MARKETING AND PROMOTIONAL PLANS FOR YOURSELF OR BY COMING UP WITH LOGICAL & GENUINE ACCUSATIONS, IF ANY, FOR THE RIVALS)

Your shrewd team has to keep on devising methods for disturbing your rivals and their market position. The leading companies do it in various ways. Sometimes they suddenly come up with certain promotional plans by declaring contests / challenges / countrywide shows or other events etc. These activities immediately disturb the competitors and they are forced to follow them, otherwise the pioneering firm alone emerges as a winner with enhanced popularity, which has direct impact on sales. So the rivals will also have to follow it without a comprehensive plan developed well in advance. Moreover the rivals will have to make some shifts / adjustments in budgetary allocations for this sudden step that would result in financial crises for other marketing activities.

Another popular way to disturb your competitor is through making certain type of logical accusations time to time on which you can stand for the time being. Accusing a soft drinks brand of having bacterial or objectionable contents in it's drinks; accusing a chain of restaurants of using non vegetarian contents in its vegetarian menus etc. are some of the examples. But for all these things you need to have a concrete base on account of which you can make the accusation.

Disturbing your competitor is a matter of your strength and conversely, you also should always be ready to face any this kind of situation created by your rivals.

Shrewd Marketing Level V

64. PUBLICIZING THE MARKET INCONSISTENCIES EXTENSIVELY AS A STRATEGY TO STOP THE COMPETITORS FROM TAKING NEW AND PROACTIVE STEPS

If you have a better information system, you always have many advantages in the short as well as in the long run. Whenever you come to know through your information system regarding some market inconsistencies, you must firstly prepare yourself for this situation properly. You can surely stop the aggressive plan that you had developed for the moment. Postpone them till a situation of normalcy arises. But during the period of inconsistency one will have to act very cleverly. It entirely asks for a different strategy to work in this situation. Remember there are possibilities that your rivals will also have an idea about the unsought and unpleasant situation that is going to arise in the market due to various reasons like changes in some of the factors that affect business etc. , but in order to get an edge over them even in this situation, a smart company tries to create panic by publicizing the negative effects of this market disturbance on the industry. As a result, a feeling of apprehensiveness and a state of confusion get developed at the rival's place; it further leads them in not going for new and proactive marketing strategies for the time being. And because you are well prepared and you have developed some contingency strategy quickly, so your performance is not disaffected in such an adverse situation. It is to be noted that a time comes when every player will act in same way by developing quickly made contingency strategies for their survival. At that juncture, only those players will survive whose SM strategies are developed in the best possible way by contemplating over every lever of markets with a pragmatic approach.

65. KEEP ON UPDATING THE COMPETITOR ANALYSIS METHODS TO EXERCISE DOMINANCE OVER RIVALS (THROUGH BETTER UNDERSTANDING THE CUSTOMERS)

The market experiences and its variations always give better insights and new directions to different market players for thinking of a better competitive strategy all the time. This results in a market having too many smart players. Now there have to be some leaders even in this situation. A highly competitive company should act smartly at this point of time with much conscience. It should regularly update its competitive analysis methods that becomes possible only by better defining and understanding the customer every next time. Every time it is found to have some refinement and improvements in customer's expectations and in it's tastes & preferences. When it is practically analyzed and properly cared for— it guides a firm in designing an improved competitive strategy that focuses on satisfying the customers in a way better than the previous one which is ultimately aimed at ascertaining an edge over the competitors.

66. WHEN YOU PLAN TO BE MORE MARKET FOCUSED, COMMUNICATE IT PROPERLY THAT EARLIER YOU WERE FOCUSING MORE ON OTHER SIGNIFICANT MARKETING ASPECTS

There are times when your marketing team suggests to get your company be more market focused. This is done to fulfill certain new marketing objective that varies from organization to organization. Today marketers are using all the possible routes for having a sustainable growth. One of the methods for this is – whenever you intend to rush to a market focused approach, you need to let it know very clearly to your customers. Communicate it in a way that earlier the company was emphasizing only on other aspects like quality, features etc. ; but now your strategies will also focus directly on development of a healthy and competitive market. Make it clear that now you are taking steps to make everyone associated with you like customers, suppliers, channel partners etc. happy and satisfied. It earns your brand lots of respect and enthusiasm from the society that finally gives you a privilege of getting considered during a customer's buying process. It is necessary to communicate that way to leave more impact of your this strategy; if you do not communicate it in such manner, it will be considered to be simply one more strategy of yours which shall not have an enduring and long lasting impact on the minds of customers.

67. KEEP REGULAR WATCH ON COMPETITOR'S SMART MOVES; TRY TO UNDERSTAND THE ACTUAL INTENTION BEHIND THIS AND REACT ACCORDINGLY

You are aware of the fact that every player of the market tries to have a larger market share. This urge motivates the companies to develop strong and rational marketing strategies. Sometimes these marketing strategies intend to increase the sales, while sometimes they are intended to beguile the rivals. Promotional strategies are normally followed by better promotional strategies. But strategies like, just making declarations in the market that you are going to increase your market share by certain percent in next five years by offering the products at highly competitive prices, by offering the channel partners the maximum commissions/margins and through heavy advertisements— creates a situation of panic among the competitors and they find themselves in a situation of perplexity. The competitors start thinking that how will you actually convert your announcements in reality. They will try to be over cautious towards your current and future moves. Rival's top management will remain worried for sometime and its concentration on the upcountry markets will witness some laxity. This will give you an opportunity to expand your market share in a market where you were earlier finding it difficult to enlarge the customer base due to rival's aggressive strategies.

68. IT IS EASY TO ATTACK ON THE COMPETITOR'S WEAKNESSES, LEARN TO ATTACK ON THE COMPETITOR'S STRENGTHS

It is very easy to attack on the weaknesses of your competitors. The weaknesses can be in the features of the product or that can be in terms of dealing with the intermediaries etc. You can easily take the advantage of these kinds of drawbacks. Once you have attacked on the competitor's weaknesses, you need to learn attacking on their strengths. For example, you can break the hard working and well performing channel partner's association with your rival and make him work for you by offering better margins and other facilities in a way explained in earlier strategies of this book. It is an ordinary phenomenon in today's markets to break association of distributors / dealers from rivals. Similarly excellent market performers at your competitor's place should be called upon to work with you. There can be so many other ways to attack on your rival's strengths. You just have to identify them for your industry in a SM way i. e. very carefully, and get it implemented rationally. The need is to list out their strengths and then it should be contemplated as to how these strengths can be handled and responded so that they no more remain the strength of the competitor.

69. MAINTAINING YOUR PRODUCT ACCEPTABLE ALL THE TIME

Ever increasing customer demand necessitates the companies to continuously upgrade the features of the product in the excessively competitive markets. Market leaders always keep a regular watch on the developments &

changes /modifications /improvements in the products and on other market forces. They keep on studying different product related issues in terms of quality, other prominent features etc. where further improvements are possible. When rivals are already showing signs of improving their products, it must propel you for quicker reactions and you must make your product a better product as per changed market conditions. You have to keep on adding value to your product continuously if you want your product to stay, either by taking the initiative or by following competitor's moves. But in any case you have to act this way; so it is better to be the first in making improvements so as to have some competitive advantage and to enjoy the image of the company as an innovator and that of a company which keeps on devising new methods of satisfying it's customers.

70. SERVICE ASPECTS HAVE TO BE AMELIORATED EVERYDAY, WHICH SOMETIMES REQUIRES HARD STEPS

Companies in the industries like consumer durables, automobile etc. are required to be extremely cautious on service aspects. Once a customer buys your product, he needs/ expects a good after sales service from you. Companies normally serve their customers through different service centres spread across the cities in a country. It is your responsibility to ascertain that these service centres are providing excellent services to your customers everyday. If at any point of time you feel that a particular service centre is not able to render enough satisfaction to your customers, you do not hesitate from taking even stern actions. You can change the service centre, or you sack the employee at that service centre who is the main cause of trouble to your customers. Regular and continuous training of the service centre employees is a popular practice for ascertainment of ultimate customer satisfaction in recent times.

71. A COMPANY MUST BE SKILLED AT MANAGING MARKETING ACTIVITIES EFFICIENTLY

You must be able to organize your marketing activities in a way that yields optimum results. The organizational structure has to be designed according to the size and budget of your marketing plans. In any case your marketing force has to perform the marketing activities in the best possible way without being unethical. The top management has to keep one thing in mind while evolving marketing strategies that the marketing people must be able to carry on the activities efficiently and with ease in maximum cases. A well developed marketing strategy is the bedrock of an organization's growth, while it's proper implementation at workplace and in the markets through your efficient marketing people are the means to ensure your success in the industry.

72. THE TECHNOLOGICAL ADVANCEMENTS MUST BE USED AT EVERY LEVEL OF MARKETING ACCORDING TO A FIRM'S CAPACITY

Today a company has to use the latest technology if it wants to achieve the level of maximum productivity on account of the overall business activities being performed by it. It is always strongly recommended to use the latest technology for manufacturing purposes. Simultaneously, in preparation of management information systems and designing of different decision support systems, for routine reporting to the senior authorities, for establishment of a proper communication system inside and outside an organization, and for all other business purposes it is extremely important to use the technological advancements taking place every now and then.

In this context, you are guided by your competitors also sometimes. Whenever You find your competitors using advanced technology for the above mentioned purposes and you have a feeling that they have been getting good results coming out of it ; in this situation you are also suggested to go using the latest technology in the way rivals are using it and if possible then in a better way. Technology is one of the significant factors which you would find as a main reason for the difference between the performance and market share of a leader and those of a follower.

73. TRY TO HAVE CERTAIN SALEABLE FEATURES IN YOUR PRODUCTS / SERVICES WHICH IMPART A SENSE OF FULFILLMENT INSTEAD OF GIVING MERE SATISFACTION TO THE CUSTOMERS

In today's perfectly competitive markets, every player continuously tries to have saleable modifications in products / services it is offering. A leader here ascertains to have certain features that impart a sense of 'fulfillment' that has greater importance than the term 'satisfaction'. Like in financial sector a customer buys a product from a company and he gets a number of additional benefits that he had not expected, it ultimately gives him a feel of fulfillment. For example when a customer buys a life insurance product, he is offered many other accidental benefits which are named as riders by some of the companies. Similarly there are several restaurants in good cities throughout the world where customer can come and have good food. But in every city there are only few places where customers rush for having food that gives them a feel of complete satisfaction. Like a customer goes to a restaurant where his kids are given some free gifts and chocolates or likewise, it delights him and he tends to come here again and again. In whichever industry you are, you should try to develop your products / services to that extent which possesses an ability to fulfill your customers—which is beyond the purview of mere satisfaction. You just should try to think of something extra / additional for the customers whenever you are to develop your marketing strategies.

74. CREATING OPPORTUNITY FOR YOUR PRODUCTS (THROUGH INTERMEDIARIES TRAINING AND EDUCATION)

There is always a place for the products of a good marketer in the markets. For a leader it becomes quite significant to conduct some leadership activities that actually arise from the fact that all players of the markets attack leaders knowingly or unknowingly. While leaders are already in top position due to their excellent marketing and other business artifices. Once they start dominating in the market, small and other powerful players challenge their leadership position by working smartly through advertisements and by putting in hard work in upcountry markets through the marketing and sales forces. In this situation, one of the most commonly practiced strategy by the leaders is to keep on educating and training the intermediaries for sales growth. You can observe this at almost every store where retailer or his sales staff would be trying to convince you that the product of a particular brand is the best in the segment. The retailers try to impose the judgment on the customers that this particular product is really very good. He gives you a self and instantly developed verbal sales report also that maximum customers are buying only this product.

This kind of language by the intermediaries and their sales staff is possible only through quick and short training to them which is further supported by reasonable incentives and continuous efforts for increasing demand of the product through pull route.

Leaders, followers and challengers can use this strategy differently. If you are a leader then act as per above. If you are not, then use this strategy by training your retailers to say words like—"you must have used other products, now you just use this brand once and feel the difference. Believe me you will always use only this brand, etc. "But here also you will have to offer some additional benefits to your intermediaries. These kind of words can be very easily heard at any store where retailers keep on advocating a certain brand in every segment. As a shrewd marketer one must use this strategy for one's products / services.

75. HAVE YOUR BRAND AN IMAGE THAT IT ALWAYS KEEPS ON RESEARCHING THE NEW WAYS TO SATISFY THE CUSTOMERS ; CUSTOMERS WILL NOT ONLY BUY YOUR PRODUCT, BUT THEY WILL ALSO WAIT FOR YOUR NEW MOVES

Leaders most of the time make efforts to establish their brands with an image that they always keep on devising new and innovative ways of satisfying the customers. These days companies are developing different type of clubs. If you buy the product/service of that company, you automatically become member of that club / privileged group. Time to time different events are organized for these club members; or in certain mega events organized by some other agencies, these members are offered some discounts.

Similarly in confectionaries industry, Chocolates were earlier promoted as kids products, then it was promoted as something offered as exchange of love, then a gift product, then it became a celebration product and so on. The product is same but its image kept on developing as per the marketer's intentions.

Similarly, it has been experienced in the durables industry that customers wait for the marketer to come up with new features or schemes etc. in certain cases. For example a customer willing to buy a refrigerator during winter season waits for sometime with a hope that the companies might slash prices during this season as the product is more useful in summer season.

76. YOU MUST KNOW WHEN TO ATTACK AND WHEN TO STOP ATTACKING YOUR COMPETITORS

Attacking strategies need lots of attention and may require some handsome monetary contributions. Your Shrewd Marketing Team(SMT) have to go through proper analysis while resorting to attacking strategies. It is necessary to study the ramifications and the benefits the organization will have in terms of increase in sales volume or improvement in brand image etc. After studying all these aspects rationally, the team should make decisions as to whether rival's weaknesses / strengths should be attacked or not.

An aggressively operating organization has to always recognize the right time when their attacking strategies are supposed to come to a standstill. It makes the calculations that already enough attacking efforts have been taken and ; now other players have also started acting cleverly and saleable modifications are taking place everywhere in rival's products because this is how competitors retaliate to these attacking strategies ; at this point of time the aggressive organization in the above discussion should also concentrate on ascertaining product suitability currently by focusing on developing the features as per or beyond market standard / expectations and ; simultaneously it should use a brake on its attacking strategies for the time being. And again after sometime, after proper analysis, attacking strategies are formulated and implemented passionately. This is how marketers work in the highly competitive markets.

77. THE MOST IMPORTANT SUCCESS ASCERTAINING FACTORS (SAF) OF EVERY INDUSTRY ARE KNOWN TO EVERY PLAYER; BUT THE COMPANY THAT IS MOST CLEVER IN EXPLOITING THE SAF WILL EMERGE AS THE LEADER

There are normally many players in almost every industry barring a few. These players know very well that what are the Success Ascertaining Factors (SAF) of their industry. For example in fast moving consumer goods industry the SAF are – various schemes being offered to channel partners , a focus on heavy and creative advertisements etc. This is very well known to every player, but only those player will be successful who possess the adroitness of exploiting the SAF properly because just knowing the SAF is not enough, implementation is important.

There are times when companies keep on behaving in a haphazard way without recognizing the SAF of their industry. It requires lots of analytical ground work in properly identifying these factors. You may have to go to proven experts of the industry or specific market research can also help you out or you can even learn from the leaders also that what are factors on which they are concentrating most. Remember the destiny of your marketing programs largely depend upon the fact that how well you have recognized your SAF and how well you have planned to exploit & control the Success Ascertaining Factors of your industry through different marketing and business strategies.

78. MARKETERS SHOULD BE ABLE TO VISUALIZE THE CUSTOMER'S WANTS THAT HAVE NOT ACTUALLY ARISEN YET AND WHICH ARE FAR BEYOND CUSTOMER'S CURRENT EXPECTATIONS

A marketer who wants to have an edge over competitors, who wants to have a strong customer relationship for a long time, who wants to cater the customers with love and respect—that marketer always goes for some extraordinary ways of upgrading the offerings and their variants. A good marketer has to necessarily have the ability to foresee the customer's wants and needs that might arise in near future. For example in Information Technology sector, companies are coming up with products tailored to fulfill your certain future needs. For example, When you engage a renowned IT company for a particular project, you normally give them details about your exact requirements and other specifications or reservations. But the marketing and technological experts at these IT companies analyze the trends and the whole situation and then they list out a number of additional aspects/features that might be needed by you in future which is related to your current requirements .or that can be useful for the industry in which you are working. And then the product is developed for you with many features that you had actually not requested for, although these features have great utilities for your business.

Similarly, a customer normally knows that his child needs cereals. And you are a company manufacturing and/or marketing cereals and possess an ability to serve this customer. But if you want to establish an enduring relationship with your customers, you will have to think even those needs which are not being immediately felt by the customers. You can go on acting smartly by informing your customers that apart from the cereal, it is necessary for your children to develop different tastes also and that is why your company has developed many variants. First day children should be given cereal with wheat contents, another day they should be given cereals with rice contents and so on. Customers should be suggested to have all the variants at home and serve it alternatively to children so as to have their children's tastes developed. With experience and passage of time, it normally becomes a need of every customer to have all these. A shrewd marketer always tries to remain ahead in terms of understanding the needs of customers than the customers themselves.

79. SHORT, QUICK AND FEW SENTENCED SHREWD TRAINING TO THE CUSTOMERS AT THE SALES POINT FOR THEM TO BE CAUTIOUS ABOUT RIVAL'S PRODUCTS

A shrewd marketer motivates its retailers with some monetary or other benefits to impart a short, quick and few sentenced training to customers at the sales point regarding the features not present in the rival's products. If a retailer educates a customer this way, it so happens that the customer starts feeling lots of uneasiness in buying that product which is not having these features. He at that particular point perceives your rival's product as an incomplete product and he normally remains with no option but to consider your product seriously subject to the fact that he does not have any reservations / penchant towards your rival's brand.

Guide you retailer in a way that whenever a customer comes, he should quickly estimate the customer's knowledge level about the product by asking the requirements in brief. Ordinary customers have knowledge about only basic utilities and/or features of a particular product. Your retailer keeps on explaining certain features that your products have but your rival's products don't have. Then the retailer can further give information regarding some new features / attributes of the product that customer did not know at all. It happens mostly in case of mechanical/electronics products where a retailer or dealer is heard to be saying to a customer that if such and such features are not present in a product, it can have numerous problems and he explains the customer in detail about the nature of problems that might arise. The customer is then left to take the decision—in most of these situations the product gets advantage, which is advocated by the channel partners at the sales point.

80. EVERY PERFORMER AT YOUR ORGANIZATION MUST BE PROMOTED ON TIME AND HE SHOULD BE CLEVERLY INSTRUCTED TO DEVELOP OTHERS ALSO AS PERFORMERS

The employees who are performing superbly well, must be promoted on time in terms of both— designation and remuneration. It does not give them an opportunity to think of job changes. They will work with full loyalty at your place only. These days it is very difficult to retain well performing employees without caring for their growth and future aspects. You always come across the figures achieved by your different employees. Whoever is excelling, get him promoted. Offer something extra like improvement in basic and recreational facilities, employment opportunities for his spouse or children etc. At the same time impart him a responsibility that his team should also achieve the figures as per the proportion in which he himself was achieving at his earlier position. This is his responsibility in addition to the totally new responsibilities of his new elevated position. This way, he will develop the team and motivate the members by guiding them to act smartly. After a certain period of time you will find many well performers in your organization. Keep on repeating the process again and again. It will convert your organization into one which is full of leaders and which has the best professionals in the industry.

81. THERE MUST BE A SYSTEM TO MEASURE THE IMPACT OF EVERY MARKETING EFFORT

Your top level management must devise a

system for measuring the impact of every marketing effort being undertaken by the organization. For this, you will have to study analytically the tentative duration of the effects and impacts of different marketing programs. At the end of every duration, you must compare the impact with the forecasted one. If it is not up to the mark, then where did your plans go wrong? Study them carefully and devise & implement an improved marketing program. After a certain period, you will be in a position to have every marketing plan implemented successfully accruing huge and optimum returns on every marketing activity you are going for.

82. KEEP ON ORGANIZING TRAINING AND DEVELOPMENT PROGRAMS FOR YOUR EMPLOYEES PERIODICALLY

It is extremely important to understand the fundamental psychology of your employees. They are also human beings. Today every employee desires to have a bright future and with passage of time he wants to reach to the self actualization stage of Maslow's theory. Most of the leading companies therefore organize training and development programs for their employees on a periodical basis. These programs aim at the knowledge up gradation of the employees which further brings a sense of fulfillment among the employees. It is quite common in the current market place that employees quite often change the jobs simply to have a better opportunity for competency development. Your employees should never get a feel that now there is nothing to learn at your organization and; whatever they had to learn, they already learnt—once this feeling arises in your employee's mind, he will start looking for a change. Many organizations today are ignoring this fact because of which they are forced to meet a situation where it is extremely difficult to retain employees.

83. YOU CAN SURVIVE IN TODAY'S SCENARIO ONLY IF YOU KEEP ON EXPANDING YOUR OPPORTUNITIES

A market gives opportunity to all the players. Once you have established yourself as strong brand in the market, you would keep on getting business according to the efforts you already have made. Now that you have a good market share, you can further increase your market share upto a certain level only. But a firm has to have growth every quarter if it wants to grow continuously for having more and more market capitalization. For achieving this growth, it is significant for the company to expand the opportunities in the newer dimensions. If you produced using latest technology standards. All these things ultimately create an urge among the customers to use/possess this product. This is how marketers try to attain a dominating position by leaving the customers with no choice but to buy the product of their brand.

86. MARKETING STRATEGIES SHOULD HAVE SOME PROVISIONS TO QUICKLY FINISH THE WEAK AND NEW COMPETITORS, SO THAT ONLY STRONG ONES REMAIN TO BE ATTACKED

While developing the marketing strategies for a particular product, you must try to contain certain provisions that would enable you in responding tactfully when a new and weak player enters into your industry. In this situation you suddenly become more aggressive in executing your marketing functions. You can quickly come up with new promotional schemes for your products; you can introduce new schemes for your channel partners; new, popular and creative advertisement strategies can be adopted– all these activities when performed suddenly and simultaneously leave such a strong impact on the market that the new player will find itself nowhere in front of you. Every intermediary will ask for similar or better schemes from the new player, which would be difficult for him to provide at the moment.

Thus you must have certain conceptual and budgetary provisions in the marketing strategy itself so as to create a difficult situation for the new and weak entrants at the moment they try to enter in your industry.

87. HAVE SOME STYLE/FEATURES THAT RIVALS DON'T HAVE

Leaders always possess some attributes that are unique to them; but mind it that it is not their Unique Selling Proposition, because USPs are copied or challenged with a better USP. Your product can have some difference; your presentation can have some difference; you as CEO or as owner of the company can act in an innovative way. For example you can see the owner of a reputed global Airlines uses unique publicity methods; he himself visits in different bohemian attires and always opts for a unique approach to publicity.

Similarly, your services can have some marginal betterment, but in anyway you must ascertain that your research team always keeps on devising new strategies that place you in a position where you have something that none of your rivals have. It gives a genuine reason to the customer to buy your product. But it is to be understood carefully that this is not the only enough reason to convince the customer